The Genius Of

THE ANCIENT EGYPTIANS

CLEVER IDEAS AND INVENTIONS FROM PAST CIVILISATIONS

SONYA NEWLAND

W

FRANKLIN WATTS

LONDON • SYDNEY

Franklin Watts

First published in Great Britain in 2019 by
The Watts Publishing Group

Copyright © The Watts Publishing Group, 2019

Produced for Watts by
White-Thomson Publishing Ltd
www.wtpub.co.uk

Editor: Sonya Newland
Designer: Steve Mead
Consultant: Philip Parker

ISBN: 978 1 4451 6119 8 (HB)   978 1 4451 6120 4 (PB)

10 9 8 7 6 5 4 3 2 1

Franklin Watts
An imprint of
Hachette Children's Group
Part of The Watts Publishing Group
Carmelite House
50 Victoria Embankment
London EC4Y 0DZ

An Hachette UK Company
www.hachette.co.uk

www.franklinwatts.co.uk

Printed in China

Picture acknowledgements:
Alamy: Juergen Ritterbach 7t, Granger Historical Picture Archive 11l, 17, Peter Horree 11r, dieKleinert 21b, Barry Iverson 26; Ron Dixon: 12; Getty Images: Print Collector 14, DEA Picture Library 15, 21t, DEA / G. DAGLI ORTI 20, 24, Science & Society Picture Library 25, 28, 29r; iStock: WitR Cover, 6, 8, TerryJLawrence 5, 18, FunnyGirl 7b, LexyLovesArt 9r, Tjanze 10, Flory 13b, prill 16, shishic 19, ttatty 22, Maciek67 27b; Shutterstock: Anton_Ivanov 9l, Kostyantyn Ivanyshen 13t, francesco de marco 23, mountainpix 27t, Niall O'Donoghue 29l; White-Thomson Publishing: 4.

All design elements from Shutterstock.

CONTENTS

THE ANCIENT EGYPTIANS

Who were the Egyptians?

People began to live along the banks of the River Nile in Egypt around 9,000 years ago. As time passed, these small groups of hunters and fishermen began to settle and grow crops. In turn, these farming communities grew into villages and towns. Systems of trade developed, and by 3100 BCE a civilisation had been established that would become one of the greatest in the world.

Egyptian kingdoms

Ancient Egyptian history is broadly divided into three kingdoms: the Old Kingdom (2686–2181 BCE), the Middle Kingdom (2055–1786 BCE) and the New Kingdom (1567–1085 BCE). The country flourished in these periods. The times in between are known as 'intermediate periods'. These were years of weaker rule, when there was fighting and unrest in Egypt.

This map shows the area of ancient Egypt along with some of the key sites the Egyptians built along the River Nile.

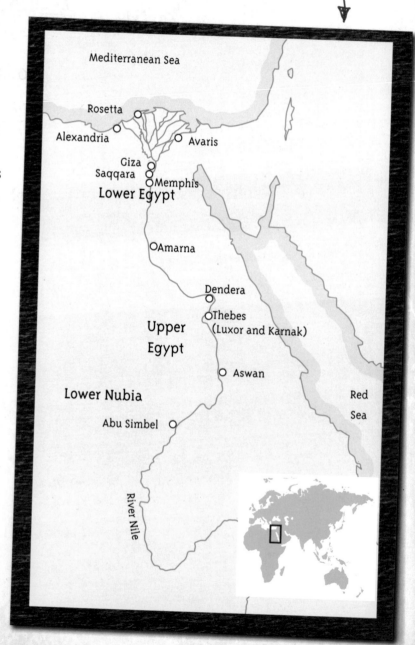

Powerful leaders

The rulers of Egypt were called pharaohs. They showed their power and wealth by building amazing temples and pyramids to honour themselves and the many gods they worshipped. For more than 2,500 years, great pharaohs such as Khufu, Hatshepsut and Rameses II ruled over a prosperous land.

Wall paintings, such as this one from the tomb of Setau, a high-ranking Egyptian, reveal a lot about the lifestyle and beliefs of the ancient Egyptians.

What happened?

Throughout this time, the Egyptians sometimes had to fight neighbouring peoples, such as the Nubians and the Assyrians. But Egypt's desert location kept it fairly safe from invaders and, for the most part, life there went on the same for centuries. Eventually, however, in 30 BCE, this great civilisation fell under the control of the Romans.

The ancient Egyptians left behind a huge legacy of information. This is contained in many different artefacts, from huge palaces and temples to paintings, hieroglyphics (see pages 10–11) and even dead bodies!

PYRAMIDS

The ancient Egyptians are most famous for building the pyramids. More than 100 of these structures have been found in Egypt. But in the days before computers, diggers, cranes and transport, how did the Egyptians plan and construct these mighty monuments?

What were the pyramids?

Pyramids were huge tombs, built as the final resting place for pharaohs or other important people. Inside were many different rooms, including store rooms and bedrooms. The interior walls were beautifully decorated with paintings, or inscribed with prayers and stories.

WOW!

The largest pyramid, the Great Pyramid of Giza, was built for the pharaoh Khufu. When completed in 2560 BCE, it stood more than 146 m high and consisted of around 2.3 million blocks of stone.

The pyramid shape represented the sun's rays coming from the sky.

Amazing architects

Ancient Egyptian architects chose the position of a pyramid carefully. For example, they might make sure that it lined up with sunrise on a certain day of the year. They also designed the pyramid to protect both the pharaoh's body and the treasure inside the tomb. Fake entrances were included to fool robbers. Inside was a maze of passages, false doors and rubble-filled rooms to put off anyone who did find their way in.

Building the pyramids

Stone for the pyramids usually came from a nearby quarry. The huge blocks were cut out and hauled on sledges across the desert. Once at the building site, the blocks were placed in the pyramid using a system of ramps made of mud and rubble. As the pyramid got higher, the ramps would be lengthened and widened to keep them stable. To fill the gaps and smooth the surface, 'finishing blocks' made of limestone were added.

This is a corridor inside the tomb of Niankhkhnum and Khnumhotep, two royal servants, in Saqqara.

Very early pyramids, like this one at Saqqara, were built with stepped sides.

TEMPLES

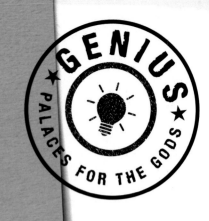

Like the pyramids, Egyptian temples were incredible feats of engineering. Nothing in the ancient world could compare with these great monuments to the pharaohs and the gods.

Four huge statues guard the entrance to the rock-carved temple at Abu Simbel

Religion in Egypt

Religion was very important to the ancient Egyptians, and they worshipped many gods. They believed that a temple was the home of the god or goddess it was dedicated to, so it was a very important place. Priests performed special rites and rituals to honour the gods and keep them happy, and ordinary people brought offerings to be made to the gods.

WOW!

The temple complex at Karnak is one of the largest religious sites ever built. This city of temples covers an area bigger than 200 football pitches!

Temples – outside and in

Some temples, such as the temples at Luxor, were built from stone blocks. Others, like those at Abu Simbel, were carved out of solid rock. Inside the temple were huge stone pillars to support the heavy roof. The walls were covered with carvings and paintings. These often told tales of the pharaohs' great victories, and showed them in the company of the gods.

The temple sanctuary was dedicated to an important god. The sanctuary in Rameses II's temple at Abu Simbel (below) contained a statue of the goddess Hathor.

Obelisks

Obelisks were tall, four-sided pillars that were placed in pairs on either side of the entrance to a temple. They narrowed from a wide base to a pyramid shape at the top. An obelisk was usually created from a single, huge piece of granite, and they were enormously heavy. No one knows exactly how the Egyptians raised them up once they had been carved!

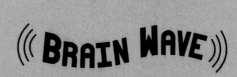

))) BRAIN WAVE)))

To avoid hauling heavy stone obelisks a long way, they were usually created at quarries on the banks of the Nile. Specially-built boats carried the obelisks along the river to the temple site.

Obelisks were associated with the sun-god, Ra. The ancient Egyptians believed that he existed within these stone pillars.

WRITING

The ancient Egyptians wanted to record important events in their world. To do this, they became one of the first civilisations to develop their language into a form of writing. In fact, the amazing Egyptians created several systems of writing, including hieroglyphics and hieratic.

GENIUS
★ WRITTEN COMMUNICATION ★

Picture writing

At first the Egyptians used pictures, called pictograms, to represent objects. As this form of writing developed it began to include more abstract shapes, which represented certain sounds. Having these additional symbols meant that people could write down things like names and ideas. These pictures and symbols are known as hieroglyphics, from the Greek for 'sacred carving'.

WOW!

The ancient Egyptian writing system contained more than 700 main hieroglyphics.

The name of a royal person was written in an oval with a line at one end, called a cartouche. This cartouche is from a temple at Luxor.

Joining things up

Alongside hieroglyphics, the Egyptians developed a cursive, or joined-up, form of writing called hieratic. The word means 'priestly writing' and it was called this because it was mainly used for religious texts. Hieratic was much quicker to write than hieroglyphics, especially as it was usually written in ink on papyrus (see pages 12–13) rather than carved on stone.

(see pages 12–13)

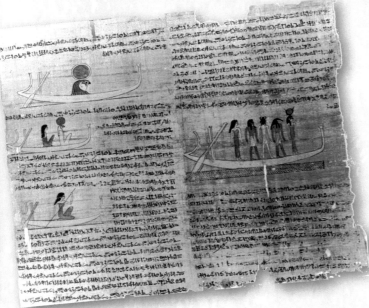

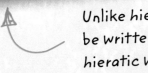

Unlike hieroglyphics, which could be written in rows or columns, hieratic was always written in rows and read from right to left.

Ancient graffiti

Examples of ancient writing can be seen all over Egypt. Hieroglyphics are carved onto pillars, columns and obelisks, as well as the stone walls of pyramids and temples. They recount the history of Egypt and its people — recording great battles, political events, prayers to the gods and praise for the pharaohs.

TEST OF TIME

For many years, no one could read hieroglyphics. The discovery of the Rosetta Stone in 1799 changed that. On this stone was the same piece of text written in hieroglyphics, a later Egyptian writing called Demotic and ancient Greek. By comparing the three, experts worked out what different hieroglyphics meant.

The text on the Rosetta Stone is an official message (decree) honouring the pharaoh Ptolemy V.

11

PAPYRUS

Before the Egyptians created papyrus sheets, people wrote on tablets made of stone or clay, or on pieces of wood or animal skin. When other civilisations discovered the Egyptians' clever invention, it caused a writing revolution.

Making paper

Papyrus is a tall plant that grows in the marshy areas along the banks of the Nile. Inside the papyrus stalk is a strong, fibrous material that can be peeled into strips using a sharp tool. To make papyrus sheets, strips from the stalk were laid out in two layers, one across the other. They were then pressed and dried. Once dried, the sheets were often joined together to create longer scrolls.

TEST OF TIME

The English word 'paper' has its origins in *pápuros*, which is the word the ancient Greeks used for Egyptian papyrus.

MAKING PAPYRUS SHEETS

1. The outer green skin was sliced off the stem.

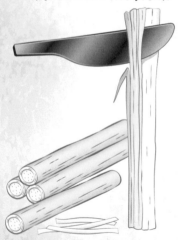

2. Thin slices of the pith inside the papyrus stem were placed in two layers, one on top of the other.

3. The layers were beaten with a mallet to help the fibres bond together.

Priceless papyrus

For 3,000 years, papyrus was a valuable commodity in the ancient world. Everyone wanted it, and the Egyptians exported it all over the Mediterranean region. This trade was very important to Egypt. To ensure that other civilisations could not make it for themselves, the Egyptians kept the method of making papyrus a closely guarded secret.

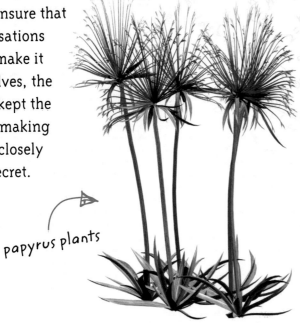

papyrus plants

The Egyptians needed something that they could use to write on their papyrus sheets. They created a type of black ink out of vegetable gum, beeswax and soot. To make different colours, they replaced the soot with a different ingredient – for example, the type of clay called ochre made a reddish colour.

Copies of the Egyptian Book of the Dead, a book of spells, were written on papyrus scrolls.

13

FARMING METHODS

GENIUS
★ EFFICIENT AGRICULTURE ★

Most ordinary Egyptians were farmers, so it's not surprising that they invented many things that helped them farm more efficiently.

The old-fashioned way

One of the most important jobs for a farmer was breaking up the soil to make it ready to sow crops. To do this, ancient civilisations including the early Egyptians used hand ploughs. Hand ploughs had to be small and light so farmers could carry them, which meant that ploughing was slow, backbreaking work.

Animal power

The Egyptians realised that ploughing would be much easier if they used animals. So, they designed a plough that could be attached to oxen. The oxen could pull a plough through the earth much more quickly than a man could. Workers would follow behind the plough, breaking up large chunks of soil with hoes. Seeds were then sown in the furrows the plough had created.

This wooden model dating from 2040 to 1750 BCE shows an Egyptian farmer with his ox-drawn plough.

Tools of the trade

The Egyptians and people from the region of Mesopotamia in western Asia are believed to have invented the sickle, a farming tool, at about the same time as each other. A sickle was a curved blade, usually made from flint, attached to a wooden handle. At harvest time, farmers moved through their fields, swinging the sickle from side to side to cut down crops such as wheat and barley. The Egytians were also among the first to make other farming equipment, such as hoes, rakes and winnowing scoops, which were used to separate grain from chaff.

TEST of TIME

Modern versions of the Egyptian ox-drawn plough are still used by farmers in developing regions of Africa and Asia.

This wall painting from a tomb in Thebes shows scenes of harvesting crops.

IRRIGATION

In the dry desert landscape, it was essential to find ways of getting water to fields to make sure crops would grow. The Egyptians came up with such ingenious irrigation methods that other cultures, including the ancient Greeks and Romans, adopted them.

GENIUS ★ TRANSPORTING WATER

The vital Nile

Every year, rains to the south caused the Nile in Egypt to flood. This was crucial to ancient Egyptian agriculture because when the floodwater went down, it left behind a rich soil that was perfect for growing crops. Good soil was important, but crops also needed to be watered as they were growing. So, the ancient Egyptians had to find ways of getting water to fields further from the Nile.

(((BRAIN WAVE)))

To keep the floodwater near their fields, the Egyptians built reservoirs out of mud bricks. These trapped the water as it receded.

The Nile flood is still an important event for the Egyptians. It is celebrated by a festival in August every year.

Canals

To control the flow of water, farmers created canals by digging trenches from the river all the way to their fields. These canals also filled up during the flood, providing a store of water and making the river more easily accessible in the dry season. However, there was still a problem. How could the farmers lift the water from the canals on to their fields? They solved this with a device called a shadoof.

The shadoof

A shadoof consisted of a long pole balanced on a crossbeam. A bucket was attached to a rope at one end, and at the other end was a counterweight. The farmer pulled on the rope to lower the bucket into the canal. When the bucket was full of water, the farmer raised it again by pulling on the counterweight. The pole could be swung round, allowing water to be poured wherever it was needed.

This painting from a tomb of the sculptor Ipuy at Luxor shows a farmer using a shadoof.

WOW!

Sometimes a series of shadoofs were mounted one above the other. This system allowed water to be raised to higher levels in stages.

counterweight

bucket

CALENDARS

The annual floods were essential to the rhythm of life in ancient Egypt. To know when the floods would take place – and to plan their farming year – the Egyptians needed an accurate calendar.

★GENIUS★
YEAR-LONG CALENDAR

Eyes to the sky

The pattern of life in ancient Egypt was based on the natural cycles of the Sun and Moon. The Egyptians used a lunar calendar, based on the phases of the Moon, to keep track of important religious festivals and events. But they needed to measure everyday life in a different way. The star they called Sopdet (Sirius) appeared in the eastern sky every year at the same time as the Nile flooded. They used this event to create a solar calendar.

The Dendera Zodiac is an ancient Egyptian temple carving showing the pattern of constellations in the night sky.

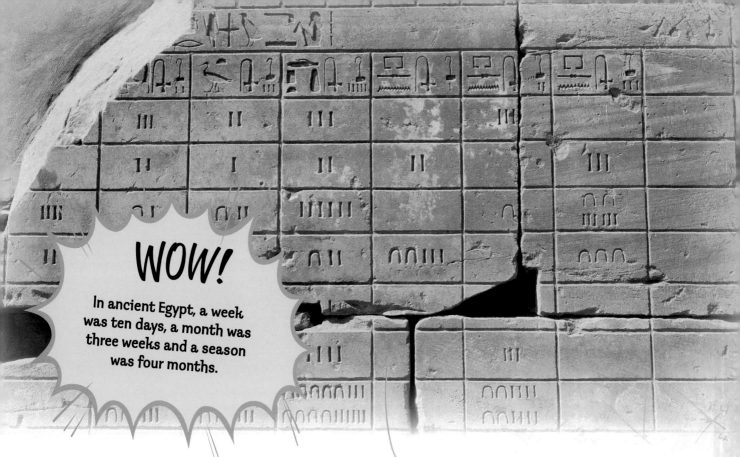

WOW!

In ancient Egypt, a week was ten days, a month was three weeks and a season was four months.

This calendar is carved on the wall of a temple in the complex at Karnak.

Three seasons

Today we have four seasons, but life in ancient Egypt was so closely tied to farming that they divided the year into three seasons. These corresponded to important periods in the farming year: inundation (the period when the Nile flooded), growing and harvest. Each season was made up of four months of 30 days. This added up to 360 days.

The 365-day calendar

The Egyptians recognised that their solar year was too short and that eventually the months would not match up with the seasons. To fix this, they added five extra days between harvest and inundation. These days became religious holidays, set aside to honour the birthdays of the gods Osiris, Horus, Set, Isis and Nephthys.

TEST OF TIME

In fact, a year is 365 and a quarter days long. The Egyptians had not accounted for the fraction, so the calendar became increasingly inaccurate. In 238 BCE, Ptolemy III added an extra day every four years. We still use this system of 'leap years', where an extra day is added to February every four years.

CLOCKS

GENIUS ★ ACCURATE TIME-KEEPING ★

Calendars helped the ancient Egyptians keep track of annual events, but they also wanted to keep accurate time on a day-to-day basis. This was particularly important for priests, because they needed to know when to perform rites and rituals in the temples.

Sunshine and shadow

One of the first methods that the ancient Egyptians used to measure time was a simple device called a shadow clock. People worked out the passing of time over a day by looking at the length and position of the shadow cast when the sun struck an upright stick called a gnomon.

Over time, the Egyptians developed these into more sophisticated sundials. An Egyptian sundial had a flat base with an upright wooden or metal bolt in the middle. Twelve lines were marked on the base, radiating from the centre. The Egyptians knew the time from where the shadow fell on these lines.

The device on the left is a sundial from ancient Egypt. On the right is part of a larger sundial — this is the gnomon, the piece that casts the shadow.

Time drips by

Using a sundial was all very well on a bright sunny day, but how did the ancient Egyptians tell the time when it was overcast or at night? They used a water clock. This was usually a stone bowl or a cone-shaped vessel. It had a tiny hole in the bottom and evenly spaced markings up the inside. The container was filled with water, which dripped out through the hole at a constant rate, so the passing of time could be measured by looking at the water level against the markings.

Many water clocks had 12 columns of markings inside, one for each month.

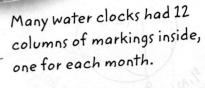

BRAIN WAVE

The ancient Egyptians used obelisks as a type of sundial. They noted how the shadow moved around the surface of the obelisk throughout the course of the day. From this they could work out the longest and shortest days of the year.

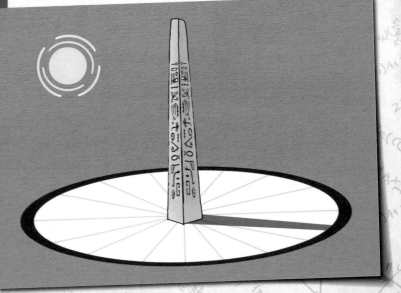

MUMMIFICATION

We know a lot about the kinds of medical problems that the ancient Egyptians suffered from. This is largely thanks to their expertise in preserving the bodies of the dead. The ritual of mummification was extremely important in Egyptian society.

Essentials for the afterlife

The ancient Egyptians believed that for someone to reach the afterlife, their body had to be preserved. So, the bodies of wealthy, important people were mummified. Afterwards, the body was placed in a tomb with all the things that the person might need in the next life, including clothes, jewellery, household items and food. Ordinary people were simply buried in the desert, where the dry sand often preserved their bodies naturally.

The ancient Egyptians believed that Anubis weighed someone's heart when they died to judge whether they could pass into the afterlife. In this scene from the Book of the Dead, Anubis is on the left and in the middle.

Making a mummy

First the body was washed, to purify it for the afterlife. Then all the organs except the heart were removed. Most of these were preserved in special containers called canopic jars, which were buried with the person.

Drying out

The body was filled with a type of stuffing and covered with a natural salt called natron. This dried out the body. It was left for 40–50 days, after which the stuffing was removed and replaced with either cloth or sawdust. Bandages were wound around the body before it was placed in a stone coffin called a sarcophagus.

(((BRAIN WAVE)))

Priests did not want to cut open the skull of the deceased person. So, to remove the brain they inserted a special hook or spoon up the nose, and pulled the brain out through the nasal passage. The brain was thrown away, not preserved like many of the other organs.

Some bodies have been so well preserved that thousands of years later they are recognisably human.

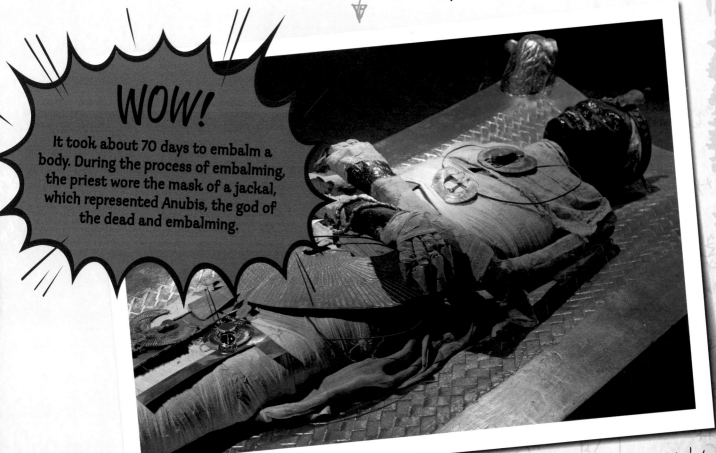

WOW!

It took about 70 days to embalm a body. During the process of embalming, the priest wore the mask of a jackal, which represented Anubis, the god of the dead and embalming.

MEDICINE

Just like people today, the Egyptians had accidents and caught diseases. Not only did they discover several new ways of treating illnesses, they were also the pioneers of a number of different surgical procedures.

Herbal medicine

The ancient Egyptians suffered from a whole range of diseases, from arthritis and gallstones to tuberculosis and tooth decay. Like many ancient civilisations, they turned to nature to treat almost all these ailments. They made medicine from plants and herbs, often mixed with wine.

This wall painting from a tomb at Saqqara shows precious ointment being transported in a jar.

WOW!

When doctors could not find any obvious cause of an illness, they would say it was caused by spirits. Spells and magic potions were used to try and drive these evil-doers away.

Healing honey

Honey was a key ingredient in many Egyptian treatments. Today we know that honey has antibacterial properties, and the ancient Egyptians noticed that putting honey on wounds prevented or cured infection. They also made a medicine out of honey mixed with wine and milk.

Surgical advances

The ancient Egyptians were the first people to set bones when they had been broken, to help them heal properly. They also performed advanced operations, such as brain surgery and caesarean sections to deliver babies. Archaeologists have even found prosthetic body parts, such as toes, made out of wood. Many surgical instruments have been discovered, including scalpels, needles for sewing up wounds, scissors and forceps.

TEST OF TIME

A papyrus document shows that the ancient Egyptians used many of the same things we use today for treating wounds. It mentions lint, bandages, sticking plaster and thread for stitches.

These knives may have been used during surgery or for hooking organs out of the body during the process of mummification.

DENTAL CARE

There were no dentists in ancient Egypt, and the Egyptians had to suffer through dental problems such as cavities and abscesses. To limit these problems, they tried to keep their teeth clean in several ways.

Mummies discovered in ancient Egypt often show signs of worn teeth and mouth diseases.

TEST OF TIME

Rotting teeth meant bad breath. To hide this, the Egyptians invented the first breath mints, made of cinnamon, myrrh and frankincense, boiled with honey and shaped into lozenges. All over the world today, people suck mints to freshen their breath.

A recipe for bad teeth

The big problem for ancient Egyptians in terms of oral hygiene was their diet. They ate a lot of bread, but they used stones to grind the flour, and pieces of grit and sand often ended up in the finished loaf! These ground down the teeth and wore away tooth enamel.

Picks and brushes

The Egyptians are also credited with inventing toothbrushes, although the Babylonians may have come up with the idea at about the same time. These ancient implements were little more than twigs with the ends deliberately frayed, but they helped remove food from between the teeth to keep the mouth healthier. The Egyptians also used toothpicks to remove food from their teeth after eating a meal.

This wall painting shows a range of ancient Egyptian food, including bread, fruit and different meats. This rich diet probably contributed to their tooth decay.

Queen Hatshepsut is thought to have died from a infection caused by an abscess after she had a tooth removed.

Making toothpaste

A key invention that helped the ancient Egyptians keep their mouths healthy was toothpaste. At first, they used ground-up ox hooves, burnt eggshells, ashes and a volcanic rock called pumice, which created a slightly gritty paste that 'polished' teeth and kept them clean. These were not tasty ingredients, though! It was only during the period of Roman rule that the Egyptians started making a nicer-flavoured toothpaste out of salt, dried flowers and mint.

COSMETICS

The ancient Egyptians took great pride in their personal appearance. Dressing well, and wearing valuable jewellery and make-up were all signs that someone was a member of Egyptian high society.

GENIUS ★ KEEPING UP APPEARANCES

All in the eyes

The Egyptians are believed to have invented eye make-up more than 4,000 years ago, and it remained a constant feature of their appearance. Their make-up was usually either black or green. Black was made from lead and green was made from copper or a green mineral called malachite. These were mixed with another mineral, called galena, to make a sort of paint.

This box contains ancient Egyptian cosmetics. The ancient Egyptians believed that make-up prevented disease, and both men and women wore it.

Wigs

Head lice could be a problem in ancient Egypt, so to keep them away people shaved their heads. To replace the hair they had lost, wealthy people wore wigs. These were woven from real hair and wool from sheep. They were set in shape using beeswax.

WOW!

Although most people wore wigs if they could afford them, priests remained bald, as it was felt they were kept pure this way. In fact, priests may have shaved their whole bodies.

Shaving implements

The ancient Egyptians also shaved their facial hair, and may have been responsible for creating the first razors. Ancient shaving implements made from sharpened stones set in wooden handles have been discovered in Egypt. Despite shaving, they also made fake beards from the same material as wigs. Pharaohs usually wore ceremonial beards — even the female pharaoh Hatshepsut was sometimes depicted wearing them in paintings and statues.

The shape of someone's beard indicated their social status. Pharaohs wore their beards with square ends.

TEST OF TIME

The Egyptians are credited with inventing the style of hand mirror still used today. These were made from metal such as bronze, which was polished to a high shine so users could see their reflection. The mirrors were often ornately decorated.

ancient Egyptian razor and mirror

29

GLOSSARY

abstract — something that does not take the shape or form of a real thing

antibacterial — describes a substance that can kill bacteria

Assyrians — people from the ancient kingdom of Assyria, which lay to the north-east of Egypt

Babylonians — people from the ancient region of Babylonia, in western Asia

Book of the Dead — an ancient Egyptian text that contained spells to help a person on their journey to the afterlife

chaff — the dry outer casing of seeds of cereal grains such as wheat

commodity — something that can be bought and sold

flint — a hard type of rock that can be chipped and shaped into sharp objects such as blades and arrow heads

furrow — a long, narrow trench in soil which seeds are sown in to grow crops in rows

hieratic — an Egyptian writing system that used joined-up symbols

hieroglyphics — the ancient Egyptian system of picture writing

irrigation — the process of bringing water to farmland in order to grow crops

limestone — a type of soft rock often used in building

malachite — a mineral with a bright green colour

Mesopotamia — a region of western Asia in ancient times

Nubians — people from the ancient region of Nubia, which lay to the south of Egypt

offerings — gifts given to the gods as a form of worship or to ask for particular things

papyrus — a tall, reed-like plant that grows along the River Nile

pharaoh — a king or queen in ancient Egypt

pioneer — someone who does something that has never been done before

prosperous — having plenty of money, food and other material things

prosthetic — describes an artificial body part made to replace a real one

sarcophagus — a stone coffin

TIMELINE

7000 BCE	People first begin to settle along the banks of the Nile.
3500 BCE	Two kingdoms of Upper and Lower Egypt exist.
3100 BCE	The kingdoms are united under King Narmer.
2686 BCE	Start of the period known as the Old Kingdom.
2181 BCE	First Intermediate Period begins.
2055 BCE	Start of the Middle Kingdom.
1786 BCE	Second Intermediate Period begins.
1567 BCE	Start of the New Kingdom.
712 BCE	Late Period begins.
30 BCE	Egypt comes under Roman control.

INDEX

FURTHER INFORMATION

Websites

www.dkfindout.com/uk/history/ancient-egypt/

www.historyforkids.net/ancient-egypt.html

www.primaryhomeworkhelp.co.uk/Egypt.html

Books

The Ancient World (Parallel History) by Alex Woolf (Franklin Watts, 2017)

The Egyptian Empire (Great Empires) by Ellis Roxburgh (Wayland, 2017)

Ancient Egypt (Technology in the Ancient World) by Charlie Samuels (Franklin Watts, 2015)

The Genius Of

Titles in the series

- Who were the Egyptians?
- Pyramids • Temples
- Writing • Papyrus
- Farming methods
- Irrigation • Calendars
- Clocks • Mummification
- Medicine • Toothpaste
- Cosmetics

HB 9781445161198
PB 9781445161204

- The Greeks • The Empire
- Democracy • Sports
- Medicine • Philosophy
- Warfare • Buildings
- Theatre • Science • Maths
- Art • Astronomy

HB 9781445161211
PB 9781445161228

- The Anglo-Saxons
- Kingdoms and rulers
- Society • Towns • Laws
- Old English • Trade
- Art • Food • Defence
- Weapons and armour
- Entertainment • Clothes

HB 9781445161174
PB 9781445161181

- What was the Benin Kingdom? • Powerful leaders • The city-state
- Professional soldiers
- Farming • Trade • Town planning • Craft guilds
- Art • Metalwork
- Working with wood
- Textiles • Botany

HB 9781445161259
PB 9781445161266

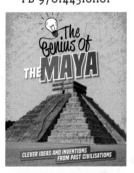
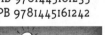

- The Maya • Government and kings • Trade • Warfare
- Cities • Buildings
- Writing • Food
- The Mayan calendar
- Astronomy • Sports
- Art • Clothes

HB 9781445161235
PB 9781445161242

- The Romans • The army
- Trade • Concrete • Roads
- Water • Calendars • Food
- The Latin language
- Government • Laws
- City services • Show time!

HB 9781445161129
PB 9781445161136

- The Stone, Bronze and Iron Ages • Stone
- Bronze • Iron • Farming
- Construction
- Settlements • Society
- Trade • Clothing • Art
- The wheel • Writing

HB 9781445160467
PB 9781445160474

- The Vikings • The Viking longship • Sails and keels
- Compasses • Exploration
- Trade • Battle-axes
- Shields • Law and democracy • Language
- Skiing • Personal grooming • Viking sagas

HB 9781445161167
PB 9781445161143